On The Job

in Construction

by Jessica Cohn

RED CHAIR
·PRESS·

Please visit our website at **www.redchairpress.com** for more high-quality products for young readers.

Publisher's Cataloging-In-Publication Data

Cohn, Jessica.
    On the job in construction / by Jessica Cohn.

    pages : illustrations ; cm. -- (On the job)

    Summary: "Have you ever thought about how all the buildings and bridges in your community get built? Who designs them? How are they built so they don't fall down? Let's learn about the jobs and skills needed to go On the Job in Construction."--Provided by publisher.

    Includes writing activity and first-person interview.
    Includes bibliographical references and index.
    ISBN: 978-1-63440-109-8 (library hardcover)
    ISBN: 978-1-63440-115-9 (paperback)
    ISBN: 978-1-937529-53-6 (ebook)

    1. Construction industry--Vocational guidance--Juvenile literature. 2. Architecture--Vocational guidance--Juvenile literature. 3. Carpentry--Vocational guidance. 4. Architecture--Vocational guidance. I. Title. II. Title: In construction

TH149 .C64 2016
690.023   2015953630

Illustration credits: p. 4, 5 (top), 7, 8, 10, 13, 16, 20, 21, 24, 28, 30: Lauren Scheuer; p. 5 (bottom): Dinardo Design

Photo credits: Cover, p. 1, 3, 8, 11, 17 (bottom), 18-19, 20, 21, 24, 25 (bottom), 27 (left, right), 28: Shutterstock; p. 4, 5 (bottom), 29: New York State Thruway Authority; p. 6-7, 10-11, 12-13, 17 (top left), 22-23, 23, 25 (top), 26 (left, right): Dreamstime; p. 14, 15: M. Hart; p. 16, 17 (top right): iStock; p. 32: Nathan Cohn

This series first published by:
Red Chair Press LLC   PO Box 333   South Egremont, MA 01258-0333

Printed in the United States of America

Distributed in the U.S. by Lerner Publisher Services. www.lernerbooks.com

0516 1 WRZF16

Table of Contents

I Lift NY super crane

Jobs in Construction

In 1955, a bridge opened on the Hudson River in New York. Fifty years later, it was worn out. Replacing a bridge is difficult and costly. But it had to be done.

Workers from all over the country have traveled to New York to help build a new bridge. Big projects like this are rare. The challenge of a big project excites builders.

"All other projects I've worked on are dwarfed by this," a manager of the project told *The New York Times*.

The parts for the new bridge needed to be carried by water to the site. The workers had to find a floating **crane** to lift the pieces. They needed a machine that could lift a thousand tons.

A Site to Behold

The builders had to bring a giant crane from California. They placed the huge machine on a barge. The flat ship traveled down the West Coast. Then, it crossed the Panama Canal in Central America. Finally, it moved north, to New York City.

Workers in the city changed some of the crane's parts. Then, they sent the machine up the Hudson River to the site. In construction, there are many important steps to follow. The bigger the project, the more details there are.

Getting a Lift
The super crane passed through the Panama Canal to reach New York. It traveled 6,000 miles (9,656 kilometers). The workers called it the I Lift NY super crane.

Super Project

The old bridge stayed in place while the new one went up. The people in charge figured that construction would last about five years. But long before then, there were many more years of planning.

A project like this brings together a number of companies. The **oversight** team includes people who work in **design**. The companies include **engineering** groups. Many people with important skills work together in construction.

⟫ You Know It!

STEM stands for Science, Technology, Engineering, and Math. These studies are key to construction. Builders need to plan and make exact measurements for fit. They need to know how materials will act.

Lasting Effects

Construction changes the area where it takes place. People who work in this industry must think about these effects. This field needs people with building skills. It needs people who can solve problems. It needs workers who can communicate well.

How do workers plan for big projects in construction?

It is important to ask the right questions before construction takes place. The teams that planned the new bridge had to think about the fish in the water. Would they be hurt? The workers had to think about the people in the nearby neighborhoods. Would the noise of construction bother them?

Talk to the Manager

"We need a responsible person," said the construction manager. "That's me!" said the worker. "Every time something goes wrong, people say I'm responsible!"

In construction, as in most jobs, humor helps people on difficult days. But the workers take their work seriously. The managers make it their business to see that things go right. They must know and follow laws for construction. The safety of the people who use their structures depends on this.

The leaders on job sites have university **degrees** in engineering. The workers have special skills and training. Every project involves "a whole team of people," says Doug Barnes. He has planned many buildings in the Midwest. Everyone on the team, he says, can "take satisfaction in his or her contributions."

New Projects

Some managers make the **budgets**. Many of them oversee workers in construction offices and on work sites. They give reports on the progress. Each worker performs special jobs, and the managers need to understand each role.

The workers are often hired as **subcontractors**. For example, a project may need people who can build an **electrical system**. A call may go out for subcontractors with those skills. There may be one manager placed in charge of these **contracts**.

Making a Bid

There are three basic ways that construction companies try to win **clients**.

1. **Lowest bid.** Companies bid on projects. They say how much money their services will cost. For some projects the company with the lowest cost can be chosen.

2. **Best value.** Clients compare both the prices and the records of the people who will do the work. They often decide based on having the best mix of both.

3. **Qualifications.** Some clients can select a company based on past successes rather than prices. Clients may consider safety records when reviewing bids.

By Design

"We shape our buildings; thereafter they shape us."
—*Winston Churchill, former British prime minister*

Important questions need answers before building begins. For example, how high can the roof be? How will the building fit into the neighborhood? Architects make these decisions. Architects study the art and science of construction.

A beautiful building affects the people who look at it. Spaces also affect the people who enter them. So, architects try to inspire people with their plans. For example, an architect will think about where the sun rises. He or she thinks about how sun will enter the building.

Chicago has four of the ten tallest U.S. buildings. Look them up!

Material Needs

"It's been very satisfying to see buildings emerge from sketches on paper," says Barnes. But the look of a building is just one part of the planning. Buildings must stand strong in many conditions. The list of concerns is long.

Barnes has worked on historic buildings in the Detroit area. The materials used when restoring old buildings need to work with the ones first used. In some places, laws cover what can and cannot be done to places that mean something in history.

Bright Idea
Marta Alonso Yerba uses gummy bears to make a material that works like glass. The architect wanted to build a wall that let light through, and she wanted the light to be colorful. So, she tried melting the colorful snacks. Now, a glass company is trying to make her new material.

Green Buildings

Right now, green building is important to many people. Green builders think about the health of people and nature. They try to protect the **environment**. So, they look for ways to avoid air, water, or noise pollution.

Green builders try not to waste **resources**. They use the same thinking for the land around their structures. For example, they may set up ways to recycle rainwater.

"It's about designing something—a world, a city, a product—that lasts," said Paula Wallace. She is the president of Savannah College of Art and Design, a school that teaches these green ideas.

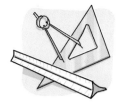

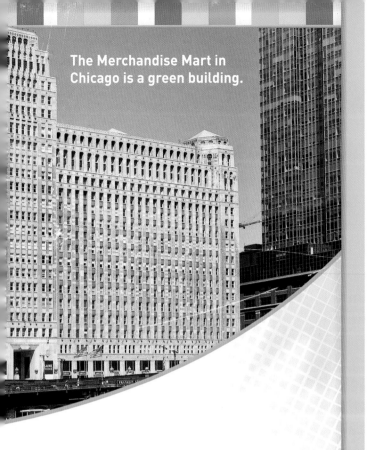

The Merchandise Mart in Chicago is a green building.

Green builders are careful at each step, such as when taking down old structures. They try to reuse materials when they can. A green building is set up to operate with little waste as well. The builders study the movement of air, water, and heat throughout their structures. They try to cut down on the resources their buildings use.

What is the work like?

An architect may start the day at a desk. She may review a plan. He may add finishing touches to a report. Then, the architect may meet with a client, who wants to go over her ideas for a new project.

Part of the job is "working with clients to develop their ideas," says Barnes. The client will want to know when a plan might be ready. The deadline needs to include the costs.

STEM studies are important for this job. Architects need to know engineering and sciences. They use advanced math for costs and measurements.

Talking to an Architect

Mathew Hart is an architect based in Washington, D.C., but his firm works all over the world. He has helped plan schools, hospitals, homes, and neighborhoods.

1 **What led you to this line of work?**

I have always loved building things and figuring out how other things worked. As a kid I built tree houses, a mini go-kart, and always wanted to help my dad with household projects. . . .

I wasn't the best art student, but I loved to create new projects, and I always tried to be better each time. Of course, I always had Legos and would build all kinds of things with them. I was never content with the basic instructions. . . .

2 **What do you like best about it?**

I love that I get to learn something new every day. Today, I am working with university administrators to design a new performing arts center in Delhi, India. Next week, I will be working on a new community center in Washington, D.C.

Each time I start a new project, I get to learn from different clients about what they do so I can design the best building for their uses.

3 **What would you tell people who are interested in the work?**

I think architecture is one of the most creative professions. . . .You get to create buildings and spaces to help people work, learn, play and live better.

Building Insight

☑ GRADE
☑ RISE
☐ ACREAGE
☐ LEDGE
☐ TRACT

"Surveyors do a lot of work by themselves, but ultimately, we're part of a team."
—Frank Lehmann, past president of California Land Surveyors Association

Engineers of many kinds weigh in with their thoughts during the planning and building stages. They help direct construction. For example, **civil engineers** work on public projects, such as dams or roads. Health and safety engineers make sure structures are safe for people.

Some engineers are experts at heating and cooling. Others know about fire protection. Certain engineers are experts at making buildings that withstand earthquakes. Surveyors measure the surface of Earth. They are needed before, during, and after construction.

⟩⟩ You Know It!

The job outlook for health and safety engineers is good, and field of civil engineering is growing faster than average.

Taking the Survey

"We are the first to show up," says Frank Lehmann. He is a surveyor in California, and now his daughter does the same work. He starts many projects by researching records. He uses the history of a spot to map property lines on a computer. Then, he will go out to see the land.

Surveyors use STEM skills and special tools to figure out the features of property. They have instruments they can aim at a distance. "We're also part of checks and balances," Lehmann says. For example, during the building of a bridge these workers will check that the structure lines up.

What do engineers say about their work?

Engineers need advanced schooling. But on sites where they share tips with one another, many say the on-the-job training has been most important. Working with numbers, solving problems, and communicating results are a big part of the job.

Engineering Assistants

Engineering assistants (EAs) support engineers in the work they do. Sometimes, the EAs keep track of the timing or schedules. They may work on files. They may make drawings.

People who are in school to become engineers can work first as assistants. Others get into this line of work after serving in other jobs. For example, someone who works in an engineering office may learn what is needed in the field over time.

>> **You Know It!**

The color of a worker's hard hat often shows the job he or she does. Managers often wear white hats.

Good Measure

Engineers need STEM skills to do their jobs well. They use computers and other tools that measure how structures and materials act. They need to understand forces such as these:

- Strain, or the stress on an object
- Acceleration, or the change in speed of something moving
- Vibrations, or shaking movements

Think about the New NY Bridge project. Engineers must plan for the vibrations and strain caused by thousands of cars and trucks crossing the bridge daily.

Path for an Engineer

Want to plan and build buildings? Have ideas that are smart and creative? Saying yes to these questions is the first step to becoming an engineer or **technician.**

Getting the Job

Skills
Need coursework that develops STEM and communication skills

Duties
Apply science and math to construction projects. Follow construction rules. Communicate plans to others. Pay attention to details. Stay within budgets.

Education
1. Need at least a **bachelor's degree** in engineering.

2. Get license and pass exams to practice. Continue classes over time.

3. May need **master's degree** to advance.

Picture This

"BIM is bringing new changes to the workplace. . . ."
—Pete Zyskowski, BIM trainer

Builders used to draw pictures of what they wanted to build. They used special paper and pencils. Then, computers became common, and people started using CAD to make their drawings. *CAD* stands for **computer-aided design.**

A line has one **dimension**—its length. A square has two. It has length and width. A cube shows three: length, width, and height. CAD helps builders draw their ideas, by showing lines and suggesting shapes.

Building Information Modeling

Now, computers can also make models filled with **data.** *BIM* stands for Building Information Modeling. BIM is a tool that fills out the models with stored information. BIM can put a building plan together by placing parts together. For example, it will put together floors, walls, and windows. The model stores information about the parts of the structure.

Teams of people can work on the models. Any small change will update the data. It used to be that changes to a design were shown on a set of drawings. Now, the information is more easily shared. A client can see a model on a mobile phone or tablet.

Building by the Numbers

A famous bridge in Peru is called the Bridge of Eggs. The whites of 10,000 eggs went into its **mortar**. The bridge was made in the early 1600s. It is still standing today.

The Empire State Building in New York City opened in 1931. It has 10 million bricks. It was the first building to be built with more than 100 floors.

The Burj Khalifa is the tallest building in the world. It opened in Dubai in 2010. The height is 2,717 feet tall (828 meters).

Before Building

Someone has to collect information on each project before it starts. He or she makes the best guess about its cost. A great deal of thinking goes into this **estimate.** The cost estimator must figure out the price of materials. He or she must add in the cost for the workers based on how long the project will take.

A cost estimator looks for ways to cut costs but keep the project safe. People who do this work often need BIM technology skills. They may make models to figure out what will happen.

After All

Before a structure can be used, it needs to be checked. **Inspectors** make reports on the work that was done. They understand how structures hold together. They look for problems, to try to keep people safe.

Inspectors also look over building plans before a project begins. They approve plans that seem to be ready. Some of these workers have special knowledge. For example, there are inspectors who know all about building elevators.

What do materials engineers do?
Some engineers are experts with materials. They test materials to make sure they will work in certain projects. Sometimes, they find a need to create new materials.

How did blueprints get their name?
A blueprint is a drawing of a structure. Back in the 1800s, builders would draw on see-through paper. Then, they shined light through it. Beneath was a special kind of paper. The light would leave white lines on a blue background after the paper was washed. Most "blueprints" are no longer blue. Now, computers can copy plans. But many people still call their plans "blueprints."

Making the Cut

"Sometimes we say we work from foundations to finish."
—Tom Ward, carpenter and union representative

Inside walls and roofs are pipes for air and water, wires, and other building materials. Beneath these structures are **foundations** holding them up. It takes special knowledge to build or fix the frames that hold it all. Carpenters design, measure, and construct these frames to fit each project.

Tom Ward is a carpenter who is based in California. He says he likes "creating things you can see, feel and touch. He says that students interested in this line of work should keep up with STEM studies such as math.

Carpenters work in homes. But they also work on big public projects. It is the carpenters who build the frames that other workers use to reach high heights. People in this **trade** also work on tunnels, dams, and other huge structures.

Inside Track

Carpenters work with other skilled workers, such as people trained to shape sheet metal and similar materials. Metal workers measure, mark, and cut metal into forms that meet their purposes. For example, they make pipes that carry air that is heated or cooled. These workers make seams where the metal meets and holes for fasteners.

25

Supporting Roles for Builders

Many kinds of workers take on important roles during a construction project. Here are just a few of them. It takes special know-how to build each system in a building, such as the pipes for running water. Here are just a few of the roles that workers take.

Plumber

Plumbers understand how water and drain pipes work. They can repair pipes and set up new ones. Plumbers can read blueprints, and they know and follow building codes. Those are the laws and rules that have been set for construction.

Brick and Block Mason

Bricks and blocks are special materials that need to be treated in certain ways. Otherwise, they can crack or stop supporting the materials above and around them. Masons have the skills and knowledge needed to build walls and foundations from these materials.

Glazier

Glass is part of most construction, and glaziers are people who understand this material. They cut and place windows. Glaziers know how to seal the edges so the windows do not leak. Sometimes, the glass they work with can be as large as a storefront.

Concrete Finisher and Cement Mason

Working with concrete requires people who know how to mix it and spread it. The material is poured while wet and allowed to dry. Finishers pour the wet cement. Masons work with the finished forms to make sturdy structures, such as walls.

Making Way

The skilled workers in construction include the equipment operators. Construction equipment can be heavy and dangerous. The drivers need to follow safety rules. The workers who run the equipment often know how to fix it, too.

Equipment operators need special **licenses** and training. Many of them can operate more than one kind of machine. Machines move heavy loads. Loading machines pick up sand and other materials with shovels or scoops. Some workers drive spreaders, such as the ones that roll over concrete to make it flat. Dozers push materials.

At Work in Construction

Concrete worker. Architect. Equipment operator. Inspector. Project superintendent. Field office coordinator. Roofer.

These and many other people work on building projects. A construction site is a busy place. Materials get picked up and moved. Machines buzz and boom. Years later, the workers can look back and see what they have done together as a team.

- Would you like to build structures you can point to with pride?
- Do you like to solve problems?
- Are you interested in piecing things together?

Think of it. You might someday work in the challenging world of construction.

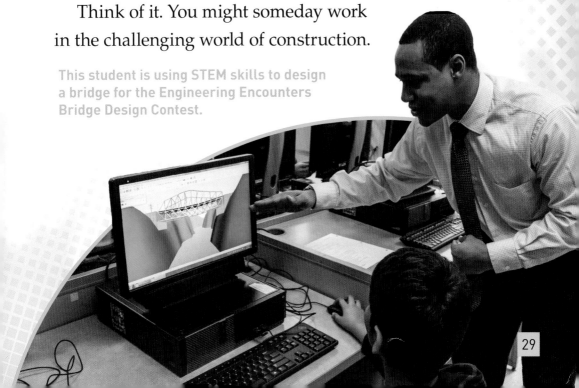

This student is using STEM skills to design a bridge for the Engineering Encounters Bridge Design Contest.

Extension
Make a Youprint!

You may not have BIM software to make drawings of a new building. But you can see how builders think. Just try making a "blueprint" of your room or classroom.

Before

Look at examples of blueprints in this book or in the library. To see other examples, ask an adult to help you find online sources.

Gather graph paper, a ruler, and a pencil. If you cannot find graph paper, regular paper will work. You can use a compass to draw circles.

During

Measure the parts of the room. Then, make a scale to use for your drawing. For example, 1 inch (2.5 centimeters) on paper could equal 1 foot (0.3 meter) in the room. So, a room that is 8 feet (2.4 m) wide and 10 feet (3 m) long would be 8 inches (20 c) by 10 inches (25 c) on paper. Draw the outline of the room. Show where the doors and other features go.

After

Think like a builder. Show where the outlets for electricity are. Show where the lights are. Label each part of your drawing.

Now, pay attention when you enter other rooms. Think about the reasons why they were built as they were. Start to think like a builder!

Glossary

bachelor's degree earned for three to five years of study after high school

budgets plans that balance costs and income

civil engineers people who design and maintain public works, such as bridges

clients people or groups that hire someone's services

computer aided design (CAD) software that makes technical drawings

contracts agreements bound by law and usually written and signed

crane machine with long arm for lifting things

data facts and figures

degrees notices awarded to people for advanced study

design in building, plan showing the look and workings of a place

dimension a measureable aspect, such as length

electrical system network that supplies, sends, and uses electricity

engineering science concerned with building or using machines and structures

environment surroundings or conditions

estimate guess as to the final cost or value of something

foundations in buildings, the lowest part, which bears the load

inspectors people who ensure that official rules are followed

lasers tools that use intense light to cut and drill items

licenses notices of permission to perform something

master's degree earned for mastery of subject at least one year beyond bachelor's degree

mortar building material that can harden in place

oversight management or supervision

resources stock of materials or other items needed

subcontractors people or groups that carry out work for another company

technician worker with basic skills needed for scientific work

technology science applied to life and industry

trade a field of work

Index

>> **Meet the Author**

Jessica Cohn has made a career of writing and editing materials for young people, covering varied topics, from social studies and science to poetry. If you ask her, Cohn will tell you that she feels lucky to be on the job in educational publishing. Each day, she discovers something new to learn and someone with an interesting story—and then gets to share the information. Jessica and her family reside in California. When not working, she enjoys hiking, helping her local library, and exploring the country.